This Dream Journal
Belongs To

Date from: **Date to:**

Contents

Welcome to the World
of Dream Journaling!

Dream Journal Entries - Record over 45
Dreams Using the Two-Page Spreads for Each
Dream

The Benefits of Recording
Your Dreams in a Journal

How to Get the Most Out of
This Dream Journal

Tips on How to Use This
Dream Journal for the Best Results

Why Do We Dream?

Types of Dreams You
May Experience

Using a Dream Dictionary for
Dream Interpretations

20 Common Symbolic Elements
in Dreams

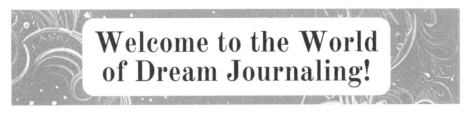

Welcome to the World of Dream Journaling!

Keeping a record of your dreams is an excellent way to explore the inner workings of your mind and unlock the hidden messages that your subconscious is trying to communicate to you.

Recording your dreams regularly can help you to understand your thoughts, feelings, and behaviors in a deeper and more meaningful way.

In this book, we'll discuss the importance of recording your dreams, the benefits of dream journaling, and how you can use the analysis to gain insights to provide a deeper understanding of yourself.

Dreams are often considered intriguing because their content can be unpredictable, surreal, and symbolic.

While we are conscious of our thoughts and actions during our waking hours, our minds can roam freely and create seemingly impossible scenarios while we dream.

Also, interpreting and comprehending dreams can be challenging, making them a mysterious and captivating aspect of human existence that has fascinated people for centuries.

While we sleep, our brains are still active, processing information, and creating scenarios that can seem bizarre, exciting, or even frightening.

Dreaming is a natural and essential part of our mental and emotional health. It allows us to process and integrate the experiences of our waking lives, release emotions, and work through unresolved issues.

See the sections at the back of this journal for detailed breakdowns of the various dream types, common symbolic elements in dreams, and more to help you get the most out of your dream journaling experience.

"A dream which has not been interpreted is like a letter unread." ~ Hebrew Proverb

Date_____   M   T   W   T   F   S   S

Thoughts Before Sleep	Emotions Before Sleep

Time Woken	Hours Slept	Sleep Quality 1-5
_____	_____	_____

Was Your Dream...?

- ☐ Normal
- ☐ Lucid
- ☐ Nightmare

- ☐ Recurring
- ☐ Prophetic
- ☐ False Awakening

- ☐ Spiritual
- ☐ Healing
- ☐ Epic

Other (specify) / Extra Info
_____

_____

Feelings Upon Wakening	Emotions Upon Wakening

Notes / Reflections / Analysis

_____

_____

_____

_____

_____

Write / Draw Your Dream

Date_____   M   T   W   T   F   S   S

Thoughts Before Sleep	Emotions Before Sleep

Time Woken   Hours Slept   Sleep Quality 1-5

_____   _____   _____

Was Your Dream...?

☐ Normal   ☐ Recurring   ☐ Spiritual
☐ Lucid   ☐ Prophetic   ☐ Healing
☐ Nightmare   ☐ False Awakening   ☐ Epic

Other (specify) / Extra Info
_____

_____

Feelings Upon Wakening	Emotions Upon Wakening

Notes / Reflections / Analysis

_____

_____

_____

_____

_____

_____

Write / Draw Your Dream

Date_____   M   T   W   T   F   S   S

Thoughts Before Sleep	Emotions Before Sleep

Time Woken   **Hours Slept**   **Sleep Quality 1-5**

_____   _____   _____

Was Your Dream...?

☐ Normal   ☐ Recurring   ☐ Spiritual

☐ Lucid   ☐ Prophetic   ☐ Healing

☐ Nightmare   ☐ False Awakening   ☐ Epic

Other (specify) / Extra Info

_____

_____

Feelings Upon Wakening	Emotions Upon Wakening

Notes / Reflections / Analysis

_____

_____

_____

_____

_____

Write / Draw Your Dream

Date_____   M T W T F S S

Thoughts Before Sleep	Emotions Before Sleep

Time Woken   Hours Slept   Sleep Quality 1-5

_____   _____   _____

Was Your Dream...?

☐ Normal   ☐ Recurring   ☐ Spiritual
☐ Lucid   ☐ Prophetic   ☐ Healing
☐ Nightmare   ☐ False Awakening   ☐ Epic

Other (specify) / Extra Info
_____

_____

Feelings Upon Wakening	Emotions Upon Wakening

Notes / Reflections / Analysis

_____

_____

_____

_____

_____

_____

Write / Draw Your Dream

Date_____   M   T   W   T   F   S   S

Thoughts Before Sleep	Emotions Before Sleep

Time Woken   Hours Slept   Sleep Quality 1-5

_____   _____   _____

Was Your Dream...?

☐ Normal   ☐ Recurring   ☐ Spiritual

☐ Lucid   ☐ Prophetic   ☐ Healing

☐ Nightmare   ☐ False Awakening   ☐ Epic

Other (specify) / Extra Info
_____

_____

Feelings Upon Wakening	Emotions Upon Wakening

Notes / Reflections / Analysis

_____

_____

_____

_____

_____

Write / Draw Your Dream

Date_____   M T W T F S S

Thoughts Before Sleep	Emotions Before Sleep

Time Woken	Hours Slept	Sleep Quality 1-5
_____	_____	_____

Was Your Dream...?

☐ Normal   ☐ Recurring   ☐ Spiritual

☐ Lucid   ☐ Prophetic   ☐ Healing

☐ Nightmare   ☐ False Awakening   ☐ Epic

Other (specify) / Extra Info

_____

_____

Feelings Upon Wakening	Emotions Upon Wakening

Notes / Reflections / Analysis

_____

_____

_____

_____

_____

_____

Write / Draw Your Dream

Date_____   M T W T F S S

Thoughts Before Sleep	Emotions Before Sleep

Time Woken   Hours Slept   Sleep Quality 1-5

_____   _____   _____

Was Your Dream...?

☐ Normal   ☐ Recurring   ☐ Spiritual
☐ Lucid   ☐ Prophetic   ☐ Healing
☐ Nightmare   ☐ False Awakening   ☐ Epic

Other (specify) / Extra Info
_____

_____

Feelings Upon Wakening	Emotions Upon Wakening

Notes / Reflections / Analysis

_____

_____

_____

_____

_____

_____

Write / Draw Your Dream

Date_____   M T W T F S S

Thoughts Before Sleep	Emotions Before Sleep

Time Woken   Hours Slept   Sleep Quality 1-5

_____   _____   _____

Was Your Dream...?

☐ Normal   ☐ Recurring   ☐ Spiritual
☐ Lucid   ☐ Prophetic   ☐ Healing
☐ Nightmare   ☐ False Awakening ☐ Epic

Other (specify) / Extra Info
_____

_____

Feelings Upon Wakening	Emotions Upon Wakening

Notes / Reflections / Analysis

_____
_____
_____
_____
_____
_____

Write / Draw Your Dream

Date_____   M T W T F S S

Thoughts Before Sleep	Emotions Before Sleep

Time Woken   Hours Slept   Sleep Quality 1-5

_____   _____   _____

Was Your Dream...?

☐ Normal   ☐ Recurring   ☐ Spiritual
☐ Lucid   ☐ Prophetic   ☐ Healing
☐ Nightmare   ☐ False Awakening   ☐ Epic

Other (specify) / Extra Info

_____

_____

Feelings Upon Wakening	Emotions Upon Wakening

Notes / Reflections / Analysis

_____

_____

_____

_____

_____

_____

Write / Draw Your Dream

Date_____   M   T   W   T   F   S   S

Thoughts Before Sleep	Emotions Before Sleep

Time Woken   Hours Slept   Sleep Quality 1-5

_____   _____   _____

Was Your Dream...?

☐ Normal   ☐ Recurring   ☐ Spiritual
☐ Lucid   ☐ Prophetic   ☐ Healing
☐ Nightmare   ☐ False Awakening   ☐ Epic

Other (specify) / Extra Info
_____

_____

Feelings Upon Wakening	Emotions Upon Wakening

Notes / Reflections / Analysis

_____

_____

_____

_____

_____

Write / Draw Your Dream

Date_____   M   T   W   T   F   S   S

Thoughts Before Sleep	Emotions Before Sleep

Time Woken	Hours Slept	Sleep Quality 1-5
_____	_____	_____

Was Your Dream...?

☐ Normal   ☐ Recurring   ☐ Spiritual
☐ Lucid   ☐ Prophetic   ☐ Healing
☐ Nightmare   ☐ False Awakening   ☐ Epic

Other (specify) / Extra Info

_____

_____

Feelings Upon Wakening	Emotions Upon Wakening

Notes / Reflections / Analysis

_____

_____

_____

_____

_____

_____

Write / Draw Your Dream

Date_____   M T W T F S S

Thoughts Before Sleep	Emotions Before Sleep

Time Woken   Hours Slept   Sleep Quality 1-5

_____   _____   _____

Was Your Dream...?

☐ Normal   ☐ Recurring   ☐ Spiritual
☐ Lucid   ☐ Prophetic   ☐ Healing
☐ Nightmare   ☐ False Awakening   ☐ Epic

Other (specify) / Extra Info
_____

_____

Feelings Upon Wakening	Emotions Upon Wakening

Notes / Reflections / Analysis

_____

_____

_____

_____

_____

_____

Write / Draw Your Dream

Date_____   M T W T F S S

Thoughts Before Sleep	Emotions Before Sleep

Time Woken   Hours Slept   Sleep Quality 1-5

_____   _____   _____

Was Your Dream...?

☐ Normal   ☐ Recurring   ☐ Spiritual

☐ Lucid   ☐ Prophetic   ☐ Healing

☐ Nightmare   ☐ False Awakening   ☐ Epic

Other (specify) / Extra Info

_____

_____

Feelings Upon Wakening	Emotions Upon Wakening

Notes / Reflections / Analysis

_____

_____

_____

_____

_____

_____

Write / Draw Your Dream

Date_____   M T W T F S S

Thoughts Before Sleep	Emotions Before Sleep

Time Woken   Hours Slept   Sleep Quality 1-5

_____ _____ _____

Was Your Dream...?

☐ Normal   ☐ Recurring   ☐ Spiritual

☐ Lucid   ☐ Prophetic   ☐ Healing

☐ Nightmare   ☐ False Awakening   ☐ Epic

Other (specify) / Extra Info

_____

_____

Feelings Upon Wakening	Emotions Upon Wakening

Notes / Reflections / Analysis

_____

_____

_____

_____

_____

_____

Write / Draw Your Dream

Date_____   M   T   W   T   F   S   S

Thoughts Before Sleep	Emotions Before Sleep

Time Woken   Hours Slept   Sleep Quality 1-5

_____   _____   _____

Was Your Dream...?

☐ Normal   ☐ Recurring   ☐ Spiritual
☐ Lucid   ☐ Prophetic   ☐ Healing
☐ Nightmare   ☐ False Awakening   ☐ Epic

Other (specify) / Extra Info
_____

_____

Feelings Upon Wakening	Emotions Upon Wakening

Notes / Reflections / Analysis

_____

_____

_____

_____

_____

Write / Draw Your Dream

Date_____   M T W T F S S

Thoughts Before Sleep	Emotions Before Sleep

Time Woken   Hours Slept   Sleep Quality 1-5

_____   _____   _____

Was Your Dream...?

☐ Normal   ☐ Recurring   ☐ Spiritual

☐ Lucid   ☐ Prophetic   ☐ Healing

☐ Nightmare   ☐ False Awakening   ☐ Epic

Other (specify) / Extra Info

_____

_____

Feelings Upon Wakening	Emotions Upon Wakening

Notes / Reflections / Analysis

_____

_____

_____

_____

_____

_____

Write / Draw Your Dream

Date_____   M T W T F S S

Thoughts Before Sleep	Emotions Before Sleep

Time Woken   Hours Slept   Sleep Quality 1-5

_____   _____   _____

Was Your Dream...?

☐ Normal   ☐ Recurring   ☐ Spiritual

☐ Lucid   ☐ Prophetic   ☐ Healing

☐ Nightmare   ☐ False Awakening   ☐ Epic

Other (specify) / Extra Info
_____

_____

Feelings Upon Wakening	Emotions Upon Wakening

Notes / Reflections / Analysis

_____

_____

_____

_____

_____

_____

Write / Draw Your Dream

Date_____   M   T   W   T   F   S   S

Thoughts Before Sleep	Emotions Before Sleep

Time Woken	Hours Slept	Sleep Quality 1-5
_____	_____	_____

Was Your Dream...?

☐ Normal   ☐ Recurring   ☐ Spiritual
☐ Lucid   ☐ Prophetic   ☐ Healing
☐ Nightmare   ☐ False Awakening   ☐ Epic

Other (specify) / Extra Info
_____

_____

Feelings Upon Wakening	Emotions Upon Wakening

Notes / Reflections / Analysis

_____

_____

_____

_____

_____

_____

Write / Draw Your Dream

Date_____   M T W T F S S

Thoughts Before Sleep	Emotions Before Sleep

Time Woken	Hours Slept	Sleep Quality 1-5
_____	_____	_____

Was Your Dream...?

☐ Normal   ☐ Recurring   ☐ Spiritual
☐ Lucid   ☐ Prophetic   ☐ Healing
☐ Nightmare   ☐ False Awakening   ☐ Epic

Other (specify) / Extra Info

_____

_____

Feelings Upon Wakening	Emotions Upon Wakening

Notes / Reflections / Analysis

_____

_____

_____

_____

_____

_____

Write / Draw Your Dream

Date_____   M   T   W   T   F   S   S

Thoughts Before Sleep	Emotions Before Sleep

Time Woken   Hours Slept   Sleep Quality 1-5

_____   _____   _____

Was Your Dream...?

☐ Normal   ☐ Recurring   ☐ Spiritual
☐ Lucid   ☐ Prophetic   ☐ Healing
☐ Nightmare   ☐ False Awakening   ☐ Epic

Other (specify) / Extra Info
_____

_____

Feelings Upon Wakening	Emotions Upon Wakening

Notes / Reflections / Analysis

_____

_____

_____

_____

_____

_____

Write / Draw Your Dream

Date_____   M   T   W   T   F   S   S

Thoughts Before Sleep	Emotions Before Sleep

Time Woken	Hours Slept	Sleep Quality 1-5
_____	_____	_____

Was Your Dream...?

☐ Normal   ☐ Recurring   ☐ Spiritual

☐ Lucid   ☐ Prophetic   ☐ Healing

☐ Nightmare   ☐ False Awakening   ☐ Epic

Other (specify) / Extra Info
_____
_____

Feelings Upon Wakening	Emotions Upon Wakening

Notes / Reflections / Analysis

_____
_____
_____
_____
_____
_____

Write / Draw Your Dream

Date_____   M T W T F S S

Thoughts Before Sleep	Emotions Before Sleep

Time Woken   Hours Slept   Sleep Quality 1-5

_____   _____   _____

Was Your Dream...?

☐ Normal   ☐ Recurring   ☐ Spiritual

☐ Lucid   ☐ Prophetic   ☐ Healing

☐ Nightmare   ☐ False Awakening   ☐ Epic

Other (specify) / Extra Info

_____

_____

Feelings Upon Wakening	Emotions Upon Wakening

Notes / Reflections / Analysis

_____

_____

_____

_____

_____

_____

Write / Draw Your Dream

Date_____   M T W T F S S

Thoughts Before Sleep	Emotions Before Sleep

Time Woken	Hours Slept	Sleep Quality 1-5

Was Your Dream...?

- [ ] Normal
- [ ] Lucid
- [ ] Nightmare

- [ ] Recurring
- [ ] Prophetic
- [ ] False Awakening

- [ ] Spiritual
- [ ] Healing
- [ ] Epic

Other (specify) / Extra Info
_____

_____

Feelings Upon Wakening	Emotions Upon Wakening

Notes / Reflections / Analysis

_____

_____

_____

_____

_____

_____

Write / Draw Your Dream

Date_____   M T W T F S S

Thoughts Before Sleep	Emotions Before Sleep

Time Woken   Hours Slept   Sleep Quality 1-5

_____ _____ _____

Was Your Dream...?

☐ Normal   ☐ Recurring   ☐ Spiritual

☐ Lucid   ☐ Prophetic   ☐ Healing

☐ Nightmare   ☐ False Awakening   ☐ Epic

Other (specify) / Extra Info

_____

_____

Feelings Upon Wakening	Emotions Upon Wakening

Notes / Reflections / Analysis

_____

_____

_____

_____

_____

_____

Write / Draw Your Dream

Date_____   M   T   W   T   F   S   S

Thoughts Before Sleep	Emotions Before Sleep

Time Woken   Hours Slept   Sleep Quality 1-5

_____   _____   _____

Was Your Dream...?

☐ Normal   ☐ Recurring   ☐ Spiritual
☐ Lucid   ☐ Prophetic   ☐ Healing
☐ Nightmare   ☐ False Awakening ☐ Epic

Other (specify) / Extra Info
_____
_____

Feelings Upon Wakening	Emotions Upon Wakening

Notes / Reflections / Analysis

_____
_____
_____
_____
_____
_____

Write / Draw Your Dream

Date_____   M T W T F S S

Thoughts Before Sleep	Emotions Before Sleep

Time Woken   Hours Slept   Sleep Quality 1-5

_____   _____   _____

Was Your Dream...?

☐ Normal   ☐ Recurring   ☐ Spiritual
☐ Lucid   ☐ Prophetic   ☐ Healing
☐ Nightmare   ☐ False Awakening   ☐ Epic

Other (specify) / Extra Info
_____

_____

Feelings Upon Wakening	Emotions Upon Wakening

Notes / Reflections / Analysis

_____

_____

_____

_____

_____

_____

Write / Draw Your Dream

Date_____   M   T   W   T   F   S   S

Thoughts Before Sleep	Emotions Before Sleep

Time Woken   Hours Slept   Sleep Quality 1-5

_____   _____   _____

Was Your Dream...?

☐ Normal   ☐ Recurring   ☐ Spiritual
☐ Lucid   ☐ Prophetic   ☐ Healing
☐ Nightmare   ☐ False Awakening   ☐ Epic

Other (specify) / Extra Info
_____

_____

Feelings Upon Wakening	Emotions Upon Wakening

Notes / Reflections / Analysis

_____

_____

_____

_____

_____

_____

Write / Draw Your Dream

Date_____   M   T   W   T   F   S   S

Thoughts Before Sleep	Emotions Before Sleep

Time Woken	Hours Slept	Sleep Quality 1-5
_____	_____	_____

Was Your Dream...?

☐ Normal   ☐ Recurring   ☐ Spiritual
☐ Lucid   ☐ Prophetic   ☐ Healing
☐ Nightmare   ☐ False Awakening   ☐ Epic

Other (specify) / Extra Info
_____

_____

Feelings Upon Wakening	Emotions Upon Wakening

Notes / Reflections / Analysis

_____

_____

_____

_____

_____

_____

Write / Draw Your Dream

Date_____   M   T   W   T   F   S   S

Thoughts Before Sleep	Emotions Before Sleep

Time Woken   Hours Slept   Sleep Quality 1-5

_____   _____   _____

Was Your Dream...?

☐ Normal   ☐ Recurring   ☐ Spiritual

☐ Lucid   ☐ Prophetic   ☐ Healing

☐ Nightmare   ☐ False Awakening   ☐ Epic

Other (specify) / Extra Info
_____

_____

Feelings Upon Wakening	Emotions Upon Wakening

Notes / Reflections / Analysis

_____

_____

_____

_____

_____

_____

Write / Draw Your Dream

Date_____   M   T   W   T   F   S   S

Thoughts Before Sleep	Emotions Before Sleep

Time Woken   Hours Slept   Sleep Quality 1-5

_____   _____   _____

Was Your Dream...?

☐ Normal   ☐ Recurring   ☐ Spiritual

☐ Lucid   ☐ Prophetic   ☐ Healing

☐ Nightmare   ☐ False Awakening   ☐ Epic

Other (specify) / Extra Info

_____

_____

Feelings Upon Wakening	Emotions Upon Wakening

Notes / Reflections / Analysis

_____

_____

_____

_____

_____

Write / Draw Your Dream

Date_____   M   T   W   T   F   S   S

Thoughts Before Sleep	Emotions Before Sleep

Time Woken   Hours Slept   Sleep Quality 1-5

_____   _____   _____

Was Your Dream...?

☐ Normal   ☐ Recurring   ☐ Spiritual

☐ Lucid   ☐ Prophetic   ☐ Healing

☐ Nightmare   ☐ False Awakening   ☐ Epic

Other (specify) / Extra Info
_____

_____

Feelings Upon Wakening	Emotions Upon Wakening

Notes / Reflections / Analysis

_____

_____

_____

_____

_____

_____

Write / Draw Your Dream

Date_____   M T W T F S S

Thoughts Before Sleep	Emotions Before Sleep

Time Woken   Hours Slept   Sleep Quality 1-5

_____   _____   _____

Was Your Dream...?

- [ ] Normal
- [ ] Lucid
- [ ] Nightmare

- [ ] Recurring
- [ ] Prophetic
- [ ] False Awakening

- [ ] Spiritual
- [ ] Healing
- [ ] Epic

Other (specify) / Extra Info

_____

_____

Feelings Upon Wakening	Emotions Upon Wakening

Notes / Reflections / Analysis

_____

_____

_____

_____

_____

_____

Write / Draw Your Dream

Date_____   M T W T F S S

Thoughts Before Sleep	Emotions Before Sleep

Time Woken   Hours Slept   Sleep Quality 1-5

_____   _____   _____

Was Your Dream...?

☐ Normal   ☐ Recurring   ☐ Spiritual
☐ Lucid   ☐ Prophetic   ☐ Healing
☐ Nightmare   ☐ False Awakening ☐ Epic

Other (specify) / Extra Info
_____
_____

Feelings Upon Wakening	Emotions Upon Wakening

Notes / Reflections / Analysis

_____
_____
_____
_____
_____
_____

Write / Draw Your Dream

Date_____   M T W T F S S

Thoughts Before Sleep	Emotions Before Sleep

Time Woken   Hours Slept   Sleep Quality 1-5

_____   _____   _____

Was Your Dream...?

☐ Normal   ☐ Recurring   ☐ Spiritual

☐ Lucid   ☐ Prophetic   ☐ Healing

☐ Nightmare   ☐ False Awakening   ☐ Epic

Other (specify) / Extra Info

_____

_____

Feelings Upon Wakening	Emotions Upon Wakening

Notes / Reflections / Analysis

_____

_____

_____

_____

_____

_____

Write / Draw Your Dream

Date_____   M   T   W   T   F   S   S

Thoughts Before Sleep	Emotions Before Sleep

Time Woken   Hours Slept   Sleep Quality 1-5

_____   _____   _____

Was Your Dream...?

- [ ] Normal
- [ ] Lucid
- [ ] Nightmare
- [ ] Recurring
- [ ] Prophetic
- [ ] False Awakening
- [ ] Spiritual
- [ ] Healing
- [ ] Epic

Other (specify) / Extra Info

_____

_____

Feelings Upon Wakening	Emotions Upon Wakening

Notes / Reflections / Analysis

_____

_____

_____

_____

_____

_____

Write / Draw Your Dream

Date_____   M T W T F S S

Thoughts Before Sleep	Emotions Before Sleep

Time Woken	Hours Slept	Sleep Quality 1-5
_____	_____	_____

Was Your Dream...?

- ☐ Normal
- ☐ Lucid
- ☐ Nightmare

- ☐ Recurring
- ☐ Prophetic
- ☐ False Awakening

- ☐ Spiritual
- ☐ Healing
- ☐ Epic

Other (specify) / Extra Info

_____

_____

Feelings Upon Wakening	Emotions Upon Wakening

Notes / Reflections / Analysis

_____

_____

_____

_____

_____

_____

Write / Draw Your Dream

Date_____   M   T   W   T   F   S   S

Thoughts Before Sleep	Emotions Before Sleep

Time Woken	Hours Slept	Sleep Quality 1-5
_____	_____	_____

Was Your Dream...?

☐ Normal   ☐ Recurring   ☐ Spiritual

☐ Lucid   ☐ Prophetic   ☐ Healing

☐ Nightmare   ☐ False Awakening   ☐ Epic

Other (specify) / Extra Info

_____

_____

Feelings Upon Wakening	Emotions Upon Wakening

Notes / Reflections / Analysis

_____

_____

_____

_____

_____

Write / Draw Your Dream

Date_____   M T W T F S S

Thoughts Before Sleep	Emotions Before Sleep

Time Woken   Hours Slept   Sleep Quality 1-5

_____   _____   _____

Was Your Dream...?

☐ Normal   ☐ Recurring   ☐ Spiritual
☐ Lucid   ☐ Prophetic   ☐ Healing
☐ Nightmare   ☐ False Awakening   ☐ Epic

Other (specify) / Extra Info

_____

_____

Feelings Upon Wakening	Emotions Upon Wakening

Notes / Reflections / Analysis

_____

_____

_____

_____

_____

_____

Write / Draw Your Dream

Date_____   M   T   W   T   F   S   S

Thoughts Before Sleep	Emotions Before Sleep

Time Woken   Hours Slept   Sleep Quality 1-5

_____   _____   _____

Was Your Dream...?

☐ Normal   ☐ Recurring   ☐ Spiritual

☐ Lucid   ☐ Prophetic   ☐ Healing

☐ Nightmare   ☐ False Awakening   ☐ Epic

Other (specify) / Extra Info

_____

_____

Feelings Upon Wakening	Emotions Upon Wakening

Notes / Reflections / Analysis

_____

_____

_____

_____

_____

_____

Write / Draw Your Dream

Date_____   M T W T F S S

Thoughts Before Sleep	Emotions Before Sleep

Time Woken   Hours Slept   Sleep Quality 1-5

_____   _____   _____

Was Your Dream...?

☐ Normal   ☐ Recurring   ☐ Spiritual
☐ Lucid   ☐ Prophetic   ☐ Healing
☐ Nightmare   ☐ False Awakening ☐ Epic

Other (specify) / Extra Info
_____

_____

Feelings Upon Wakening	Emotions Upon Wakening

Notes / Reflections / Analysis

_____
_____
_____
_____
_____
_____

Write / Draw Your Dream

Date_____   M   T   W   T   F   S   S

Thoughts Before Sleep	Emotions Before Sleep

Time Woken   Hours Slept   Sleep Quality 1-5

_____   _____   _____

Was Your Dream...?

- [ ] Normal
- [ ] Lucid
- [ ] Nightmare

- [ ] Recurring
- [ ] Prophetic
- [ ] False Awakening

- [ ] Spiritual
- [ ] Healing
- [ ] Epic

Other (specify) / Extra Info
_____

_____

Feelings Upon Wakening	Emotions Upon Wakening

Notes / Reflections / Analysis

_____

_____

_____

_____

_____

Write / Draw Your Dream

Date_____   M T W T F S S

Thoughts Before Sleep	Emotions Before Sleep

Time Woken   Hours Slept   Sleep Quality 1-5

_____   _____   _____

Was Your Dream...?

☐ Normal   ☐ Recurring   ☐ Spiritual
☐ Lucid   ☐ Prophetic   ☐ Healing
☐ Nightmare   ☐ False Awakening   ☐ Epic

Other (specify) / Extra Info
_____

_____

Feelings Upon Wakening	Emotions Upon Wakening

Notes / Reflections / Analysis

_____

_____

_____

_____

_____

_____

Write / Draw Your Dream

Date_____   M   T   W   T   F   S   S

Thoughts Before Sleep	Emotions Before Sleep

Time Woken   Hours Slept   Sleep Quality 1-5

_____   _____   _____

Was Your Dream...?

☐ Normal   ☐ Recurring   ☐ Spiritual
☐ Lucid   ☐ Prophetic   ☐ Healing
☐ Nightmare   ☐ False Awakening   ☐ Epic

Other (specify) / Extra Info

_____

_____

Feelings Upon Wakening	Emotions Upon Wakening

Notes / Reflections / Analysis

_____

_____

_____

_____

_____

Write / Draw Your Dream

Date_____   M   T   W   T   F   S   S

Thoughts Before Sleep	Emotions Before Sleep

Time Woken	Hours Slept	Sleep Quality 1-5
_____	_____	_____

Was Your Dream...?

☐ Normal   ☐ Recurring   ☐ Spiritual
☐ Lucid   ☐ Prophetic   ☐ Healing
☐ Nightmare   ☐ False Awakening ☐ Epic

Other (specify) / Extra Info
_____

_____

Feelings Upon Wakening	Emotions Upon Wakening

Notes / Reflections / Analysis

_____

_____

_____

_____

_____

_____

Write / Draw Your Dream

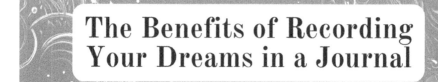

The Benefits of Recording Your Dreams in a Journal

First, it helps you to remember your dreams more vividly. Many people find that they forget their dreams within minutes of waking up, and without a record, those dreams are lost forever.

By writing down your dreams, you can preserve them for later reflection and analysis.

Second, it can reveal patterns and themes in your dreams that may be related to your emotions, thoughts, and actions. By tracking these patterns over time, you may gain insight into your innermost desires, fears, and motivations.

The interpretation of your dreams can be important for exploring your inner self and achieving personal development.

Comprehending their significance can provide you with a deeper understanding of your unconscious psyche, leading to an improved comprehension of yourself.

For example, you may identify recurring symbols or themes in your dreams that are related to emotional issues.

By addressing these issues, you may find that you feel more fulfilled and at peace in your waking life.

In conclusion, keeping a dream journal can be a valuable tool for understanding your dreams, analyzing their meanings, and reflecting on your experiences, to then gain a deeper understanding of your inner world and subconscious.

So grab a pen, and start exploring the fascinating world of your dreams!

How to Get the Most Out of This Dream Journal

After recording the date and day, there are prompts to write down your **thoughts and emotions before sleep** to see if there is any significance with how you're feeling before you go to sleep and what you dream.

Record the time you wake up, the number of hours slept, and your sleep quality, which you can score from 1 (poor) to 5 (amazing!).

Categorize your dream using the tick boxes as per the following themes (there are more detailed explanations in a later section of this book. See "Types of Dreams You May Experience"):

- **Normal dreams**: Most people experience normal dreams during their sleep cycle. These involve a range of emotions, events, and settings, including the mundane (running errands) and fantastical (flying), and can evoke feelings of joy, sadness, fear, or confusion.
- **Lucid dreams**: In a lucid dream, the dreamer is aware that they are dreaming and may be able to control or influence the dream's content and direction.
- **Nightmares**: Nightmares are frightening dreams that can cause intense fear, anxiety, and distress.
- **Recurring dreams**: These are dreams that occur repeatedly, often with similar themes or symbols, and may indicate unresolved issues or conflicts in the dreamer's life.
- **Prophetic dreams**: Some people believe that dreams can provide glimpses of the future or contain messages from the divine or the unconscious mind.
- **False awakenings**: Here, the dreamer believes they have woken up from a dream, only to realize they are still dreaming.
- **Spiritual dreams**: These are dreams that involve themes and symbols related to spiritual or mystical experiences, such as divine beings, sacred places, and receiving spiritual guidance.
- **Healing dreams**: These are dreams that may provide insight into physical or emotional healing, or offer comfort and reassurance during times of stress or illness.
- **Epic dreams**: Epic dreams are grandiose or epic in scale, often involving mythical or legendary figures or places, and may contain symbolic messages or archetypal themes.

It's easy to forget **your feelings and emotions** when you wake from dreaming, so there are also sections to record and track these.

There is a section to write down any **notes and reflections to record your thoughts, feelings, and analysis**. The more you write down and remember, the more you will get out of recording and tracking your dreams. Also use the write/draw page if you need more room.

When **interpreting your dreams**, you can add the information once you've looked it up in a dream dictionary or online, or you can include this at a later date when you've had time to **reflect on the meanings** of your dreams.

The second of the two-page spread is a dot grid page to write and/or draw your dream in as much detail as possible:

- **Try to capture every detail you can remember**: This includes the setting, people, emotions, colors, symbols, actions, sounds, smells, sensations, mood/atmosphere, and events of the dream, which all help to identify patterns and themes over time.
- **Use descriptive language**: Use descriptive language to paint a vivid picture of the dream, including colors, textures, and sensory experiences. Capturing these makes it easier to interpret.
- **Pay attention to recurring themes and symbols**: Drawing or sketching symbolic elements such as animals, water, fire, and death in your dream journal can aid in visualization, memory recall, and pattern identification, while also serving as a creative outlet to explore emotions and deepen your understanding of your subconscious mind and common dream themes such as fear, loss, and transformation.
- **Consider the emotions and feelings in your dream**: These can be an important part of the dream experience, so be sure to record any feelings or emotions you experienced during the dream.
- **Note any connections to real-life events**: Dreams may be connected to events or experiences in your waking life, so try to identify any connections or parallels between your dreams and your life.

Dream interpretation is subjective, and there is no correct or incorrect way to approach it. In addition, keeping a dream journal can enhance memory retention and the ability to recall details.

"Understanding ourselves is like solving a mystery - it requires patience, curiosity, and a lot of self-reflection."

Tips on How to Use This Dream Journal for the Best Results

- **Keep your dream journal within reach**: Place your journal and pen beside your bed, so you can easily record your dreams as soon as you wake up. This can help you to remember the details of your dream more accurately and vividly.
- **Record the date and day (and even the time if you're aware) of each dream**: This helps to track patterns and recurring themes.
- **Write down as much detail as possible**: Include the people, places, emotions, and sensations you experienced in the dream.
- **Use the present tense**: When writing down your dream, express actions or events as though they are happening currently to help you vividly recall the experience.
- **Draw or sketch any images that you remember**: Again, this will help you to remember your dreams more clearly.
- **Use keywords and phrases**: This will help you to summarize the main themes and symbols in your dream.
- **Record your dreams regularly**: Try to record your dreams every day, even if you only remember fragments or brief impressions. Consistency is key when it comes to developing a practice of dream journaling.
- **Reflect on your dreams**: After you've recorded your dream, take some time to reflect on what it may mean. Ask yourself questions such as "What emotions did I feel during the dream?" or "What symbols or themes stood out to me?" Gain insight into your subconscious mind, as well as any underlying emotions or conflicts, by reflecting on your thoughts and experiences.
- **Look for patterns and recurring themes across multiple dreams**: These may reveal important insights into your psyche.
- **Don't worry about being perfect**: Your dream journal is a personal and private space, so don't worry about spelling or grammar errors or how your writing looks. The most important thing is that you record your dreams consistently and with as much detail as possible.
- **Be patient and persistent**: It may take time and practice to develop a consistent dream journaling habit and fully explore the depths of your subconscious mind.

Following these tips can gain valuable insights into your subconscious mind and enhance your self-improvement and introspection.

Why Do We Dream?

This is a question that has puzzled scientists, philosophers, and psychologists for centuries.

While we still don't fully understand the purpose of dreams, there are many theories that attempt to explain why we dream.

One of the earliest theories of dreaming comes from the ancient Greeks, who believed that dreams were messages from the gods.

In more recent times, Sigmund Freud proposed that dreams were a way for our subconscious mind to express repressed desires and emotions that were not accessible to our conscious mind during waking hours.

He held the belief that dreams functioned as a means of fulfilling one's wishes.

While Freud's theory is still popular today, many scientists and psychologists have developed additional theories to explain why we dream.

Here are a few examples:

- **Memory consolidation**: Some researchers believe that dreams help us to consolidate and process information from our waking experiences.
  - During sleep, our brain may replay and organize memories from the day, helping us to better retain and recall important information.

"Dreams are the reality that we create in our minds while we sleep." ~ Plato

Why Do We Dream?

- **Emotional regulation**: Dreams may also serve as a way for our brain to process and regulate our emotions.
  - By replaying emotionally charged experiences during sleep, our brain may be able to reduce the intensity of negative emotions and promote positive feelings.

- **Problem-solving**: Some studies suggest that dreams may help us to solve problems and generate creative solutions.
  - During sleep, our brain may continue to work on unresolved issues and find new perspectives or insights.

- **Evolutionary adaptation**: Another theory is that dreams are an evolutionary adaptation that helped our ancestors to survive and thrive.
  - Dreams may have helped early humans to simulate and prepare for dangerous or challenging situations, improving their chances of survival.

While there is still much we don't know about the purpose of dreams, there is no doubt that they are a fascinating and important aspect of the human experience.

By exploring our dreams and reflecting on their meanings and significance, we may be able to gain valuable insights into our subconscious mind and enhance our personal growth and self-awareness.

"Getting to know yourself is like a never-ending story - there's always something new to discover."

Types of Dreams You May Experience

Normal - A normal dream is a type of dream that involves a wide range of themes, symbols, and experiences that are typical of the human dream experience. These dreams may be realistic or fantastical, and can involve elements of both the conscious and unconscious mind.

Such dreams can range from mundane experiences, such as running errands or talking with friends, to more fantastical scenarios, such as flying or encountering imaginary creatures. They may also involve themes and symbols that are unique to the dreamer's personal experiences and emotions, such as unresolved conflicts, fears, desires, or aspirations.

These dreams can have a variety of functions, including processing emotions and memories, consolidating learning and experiences, and providing creative inspiration. They may also serve as a form of self-expression or a means of exploring different aspects of the self.

While normal dreams may not always have a clear or obvious meaning, they are an important part of the human experience and may provide insights into our thoughts, feelings, and experiences. By paying attention to our "normal" dreams and exploring their possible meanings, we can gain a greater understanding of ourselves and our inner world.

***

Lucid - A lucid dream is a type of dream in which the dreamer is aware that they are dreaming and may be able to control or influence the dream's content and direction. In a lucid dream, the dreamer is conscious and able to think and reason, as opposed to being lost in the dream world without awareness.

These dreams can be very vivid and realistic, and may involve experiences that are not possible in waking life, such as flying, teleporting, or interacting with imaginary characters. The dreamer may be able to manipulate the dream environment or their own actions within the dream, allowing them to explore their fantasies and desires in a safe and controlled manner.

Lucid dreaming is a skill that can be developed through various techniques, such as meditation and visualization. Some people use lucid dreaming as a tool for personal growth, creative inspiration, or problem-solving, while others simply enjoy the experience of exploring their own consciousness and imagination.

Overall, lucid dreams can be a fascinating and transformative experience, providing a unique opportunity to explore the inner workings of the mind and expand our sense of what is possible.

*****

Nightmare - A nightmare is a particularly distressing or frightening dream that often wakes the dreamer up feeling anxious, scared, or panicked. Nightmares can include a range of different themes and scenarios, but they often involve some kind of threat, danger, or trauma.

When describing a nightmare, it's important to convey the intense emotions and sensations that accompany the dream. This may include fear, panic, dread, or a sense of impending doom.

Common themes in nightmares include:

- Being chased or attacked by a monster, animal, or person
- Falling from a great height or being trapped in a dangerous situation
- Experiencing the loss of a family member/friend or a traumatic event
- Finding that you are confined or helpless in a perilous situation
- Experiencing supernatural or paranormal events, such as ghosts or demons

When describing a nightmare, it's important to focus on the emotions and feelings experienced during the dream, as well as any physical sensations, sounds, or smells.

It's also helpful to note any details or events that may have triggered the nightmare, such as a stressful situation at work or an upsetting news story.

Overall, describing a nightmare can be a powerful way to process and cope with the intense emotions and fears that accompany these challenging dreams.

Recurring - A recurring dream is a dream that repeats itself over time, often with similar or identical elements. Recurring dreams can be particularly vivid and memorable, and they can sometimes feel like a message from the unconscious mind.

When describing a recurring dream, it's important to focus on the elements that repeat themselves. This may include the setting, the characters or people involved, the events that occur, or the emotions and feelings experienced during the dream.

Some common examples of recurring dreams include:

- **Falling**: Dreams about falling can indicate a lack of control in one's life or a fear of failure.
- **Being chased**: Dreams about being chased can indicate avoidance behavior or a feeling of being overwhelmed.
- **Teeth falling out**: Dreams about teeth falling out can indicate anxiety or a fear of losing power or attractiveness.
- **Being unprepared for an exam or presentation**: Dreams about being unprepared can indicate anxiety or a fear of failure.
- **Flying**: Dreams about flying can indicate a desire for freedom or a sense of control.
- **Being naked in public**: Dreams about being naked in public can indicate vulnerability or a fear of being exposed.
- **Seeing a deceased loved one**: This type of dream can represent a desire for connection or closure, or feeling unresolved grief or loss.

When describing a recurring dream, it's important to note any changes or variations that occur over time, as these can provide clues to the underlying meaning of the dream.

Overall, recurring dreams can offer valuable insight into the unconscious mind and the dreamer's innermost thoughts and emotions.

***

Prophetic - A prophetic dream is a dream that appears to predict or foreshadow a future event. These dreams can feel particularly vivid and significant, often leaving the dreamer with a strong sense of knowing or intuition.

When describing a prophetic dream, it's important to focus on the specific details and symbols that may hold meaning related to the predicted event. This may include objects, people, locations, or other elements that appear in the dream.

Prophetic dreams can involve a wide range of themes and scenarios, but some common examples include:

- Catastrophic natural events like floods, hurricanes, or earthquakes.
- Accidents or illnesses affecting oneself or a loved one.
- Changes in career, relationships, or other important life circumstances.
- Significant world events, such as political upheaval or pandemics.

When describing a prophetic dream, it's important to convey the sense of certainty or knowing that often accompanies these dreams.

The dreamer may feel a strong sense of conviction or intuition about the predicted event, even if they don't fully understand the symbolism or meaning of the dream.

It's also helpful to note any other signs or synchronicities that may confirm the prophetic nature of the dream, such as a sense of déjà vu or a series of related coincidences.

Overall, prophetic dreams can offer a powerful glimpse into the future and provide guidance and insight into the dreamer's waking life.

***

False Awakening - A false awakening dream is a type of dream in which the dreamer believes they have woken up from sleep, but are actually still dreaming.

In these dreams, the dreamer may experience a range of realistic and mundane activities, such as getting out of bed, brushing their teeth, or preparing for their day.

When recording this type of dream, it's important to convey the sense of confusion or disorientation that often accompanies these dreams.

The dreamer may believe that they are fully awake and going about their day, only to realize later that they are still asleep. This can be a disconcerting experience, as it can blur the line between dream and reality.

It's also helpful to note any specific details or events that occurred during the false awakening, as these may hold symbolic or mental relevance.

For example, if the dreamer repeatedly tries to leave their house but keeps getting lost or turned around, this could represent a sense of feeling lost or directionless in their waking life.

False awakening dreams can be a useful tool for exploring the boundaries between dream and reality, and can offer insights into the nature of consciousness and perception.

Overall, describing a false awakening dream can help the dreamer better understand their own subconscious processes and gain new insights into their waking life.

***

Spiritual - A spiritual dream is a type of dream that is imbued with a sense of deep meaning, insight, or connection to a higher power or spiritual realm.

In these dreams, the dreamer may experience a range of mystical or transcendent experiences, such as encountering a divine being or experiencing a sense of oneness with the universe.

When describing a spiritual dream, it's important to convey the sense of awe, wonder, or inspiration that often accompanies these dreams.

The dreamer may feel a profound sense of insight or understanding about themselves or their place in the world.

They may also experience a sense of peace, love, or compassion that transcends their waking life experiences.

It's also helpful to note any specific symbols, messages, or themes that appeared in the dream, as these may hold important spiritual significance or be meaningful in terms of mental or emotional impact.

For example, a dream about a burning bush may symbolize a powerful spiritual awakening or a call to action, while a dream about a peaceful garden may represent a sense of inner peace or tranquility.

Overall, describing a spiritual dream can help the dreamer better understand their own spiritual beliefs and experiences, and can provide a powerful source of guidance, insight, and inspiration for their waking life.

Healing - A healing dream is a type of dream that is focused on emotional or physical healing.

In these dreams, the dreamer may experience a range of therapeutic experiences, such as meeting with a spiritual healer, undergoing a physical healing, or experiencing a sense of emotional release or resolution.

When describing a healing dream, it's important to convey the sense of comfort, relief, or transformation that often accompanies these dreams.

The dreamer may feel a sense of closure or resolution about past events, or experience a sense of newfound strength or empowerment.

It's also helpful to note any specific symbols, messages, or themes that appeared in the dream, as these may hold important symbolic or psychological significance.

For example, a dream about being in a beautiful garden may represent a sense of renewal and growth, while a dream about confronting a past trauma may signify a desire for resolution or closure.

Overall, describing a healing dream can help the dreamer better understand their own emotional and psychological needs, and can provide a powerful source of comfort, guidance, and transformation for their waking life.

***

Epic - An epic dream is a type of dream that is characterized by its grandeur, complexity, and vividness. In these dreams, the dreamer may experience a range of epic or fantastical events, such as battling mythical creatures, exploring exotic lands, or engaging in epic quests or battles.

When describing an epic dream, it's important to convey the sense of excitement, adventure, or awe that often accompanies these dreams. The dreamer may feel a sense of thrill or exhilaration as they explore new worlds or face incredible challenges.

It's also helpful to note any specific symbols, messages, or themes that appeared in the dream, as these may hold important symbolic or emotional importance.

For example, a dream about traveling to a distant planet may represent a desire for adventure or a need to explore new aspects of oneself, while a dream about battling a dragon may symbolize a need to overcome inner fears or challenges.

Overall, describing an epic dream can be an exciting and thrilling experience, and can provide the dreamer with a powerful source of inspiration, creativity, and imagination for their waking life.

More types of dreams include:

- **Anxiety dreams**: These are dreams that are often related to feelings of fear, stress, or worry. They may involve scenarios where you are being chased or falling or feeling trapped.
- **Flying dreams**: These dreams are characterized by the sensation of flying or floating in the air. They may be associated with feelings of freedom, release, or escape.
- **Telepathic dreams**: Some people report dreams that seem to involve telepathic communication with other people, either living or deceased.
- **Out-of-body experiences**: In these dreams, the dreamer feels as though they are floating above their physical body, or traveling through time and space.
- **Pre-cognitive dreams**: Similar to prophetic dreams, these dreams seem to offer a glimpse of the future, but in a more general sense, rather than specific events.
- **Premonitory dreams**: These are also similar to prophetic dreams, but their emphasis lies in alerting the dreamer about imminent danger or crisis.
- **Shared dreams**: Some people report dreams that they share with others, either people they know in waking life or strangers they have never met.
- **False lucid dreams**: Dreams where the dreamer believes they are in a lucid dream but cannot actually control or manipulate the dream.
- **Transcendent dreams**: These offer a sense of spiritual or mystical transcendence, beyond the limitations of the physical world.
- **Hypnagogic dreams**: Dreams that occur during the transition between wakefulness and sleep, often characterized by vivid hallucinations or surreal imagery.

It is recommended to use a Dream Dictionary so you have a useful resource for exploring the deeper meanings and messages that may be present in your dreams. See the next page for more information.

Using a Dream Dictionary for Dream Interpretations

A dream dictionary is a reference tool that provides interpretations for common symbols, themes, and imagery that may appear in dreams.

Using a dream dictionary can be helpful for several reasons:

- **Provides a starting point for analysis**: A dream dictionary can offer a starting point for interpreting the symbols and themes present in a dream, especially if the dreamer is unfamiliar with them. By looking up the meaning of a particular symbol, it may offer new insight into the potential significance of the dream.
- **Offers a wider range of perspectives**: Dream dictionaries often draw on various sources, such as cultural beliefs, mythology, and psychology, to provide interpretations of dream symbols. This can offer the dreamer a wider range of perspectives to consider when interpreting their dreams.
- **Can help identify patterns**: By using a dream dictionary to identify recurring symbols or themes in their dreams, the dreamer may be able to recognize patterns or recurring themes in their subconscious that they may not have been aware of before.
- **Encourages self-reflection**: Using a dream dictionary can encourage the dreamer to reflect on their personal associations with the symbols and themes in their dreams, which can help them gain a deeper understanding of their own psyche.

There are numerous dream dictionaries and online resources available to aid in the researching and interpreting of your dreams.

While using a dream dictionary can be a helpful tool for exploring the meanings and messages in dreams, it's important to remember that dreams are deeply personal and subjective experiences. Ultimately, the most valuable interpretations of dreams come from the dreamer's own intuition and self-reflection...

See the next page for a list of the general meanings of symbolic elements commonly found in dreams.

"Dreams are the experiences of the soul in sleep."
~ Aristotle

20 Common Symbolic Elements in Dreams

Dream symbols have unique meanings based on personal history and culture, influenced by the dream's setting and your own associations. Consider both the emotions and experiences in the dream as a whole, as well as individual symbols.

Some common symbolic elements in dreams include:

1. **Water**: can mean emotions, the subconscious mind, the flow of life
2. **Teeth**: symbolize power, attractiveness, or anxiety
3. **Flying**: can represent a desire for freedom or a sense of control
4. **Snakes**: can symbolize fear, transformation, or temptation
5. **Houses or buildings**: can represent the self - the bedroom can represent privacy; the basement can relate to the subconscious
6. **Death or dying**: can symbolize change, transformation, endings
7. **Animals**: can represent different qualities or instincts, such as strength or cunning
8. **Bridges**: can represent transitions or connections between different aspects of life
9. **Cars or vehicles**: can represent our journey through life or our sense of control over our destiny
10. **Falling**: can symbolize a loss of control or a fear of failure
11. **Babies**: can represent new beginnings or vulnerability
12. **Nakedness**: can symbolize vulnerability or fear of exposure
13. **Being chased**: may mean stress or avoiding a problem
14. **School or tests**: can represent a desire for knowledge or feelings of inadequacy
15. **Money**: can symbolize power or a desire for material possessions
16. **Fire**: can represent passion, transformation, or destruction
17. **Trees**: can represent growth, stability, or family roots
18. **Time**: can represent the passage of life or a sense of urgency
19. **Insects**: may mean annoyances, fears, or hidden emotions
20. **Masks**: can represent deception, hiding one's true self, or the desire to be someone else

Thank you for choosing this dream journal. We hope that the process of recording your dreams has been both interesting and beneficial to you!

"Dreams can reveal hidden truths about ourselves and the world around us."